Palding
AF323019
116203
Yellowstone River
IndependenceRock
Prings
Ft Hall
SodaSprings
South Pass
North
Ft Platte
Big Bear River
Platte
Salt Lake
Ft Bridger
Ft Laramie
Creene R
South Platte

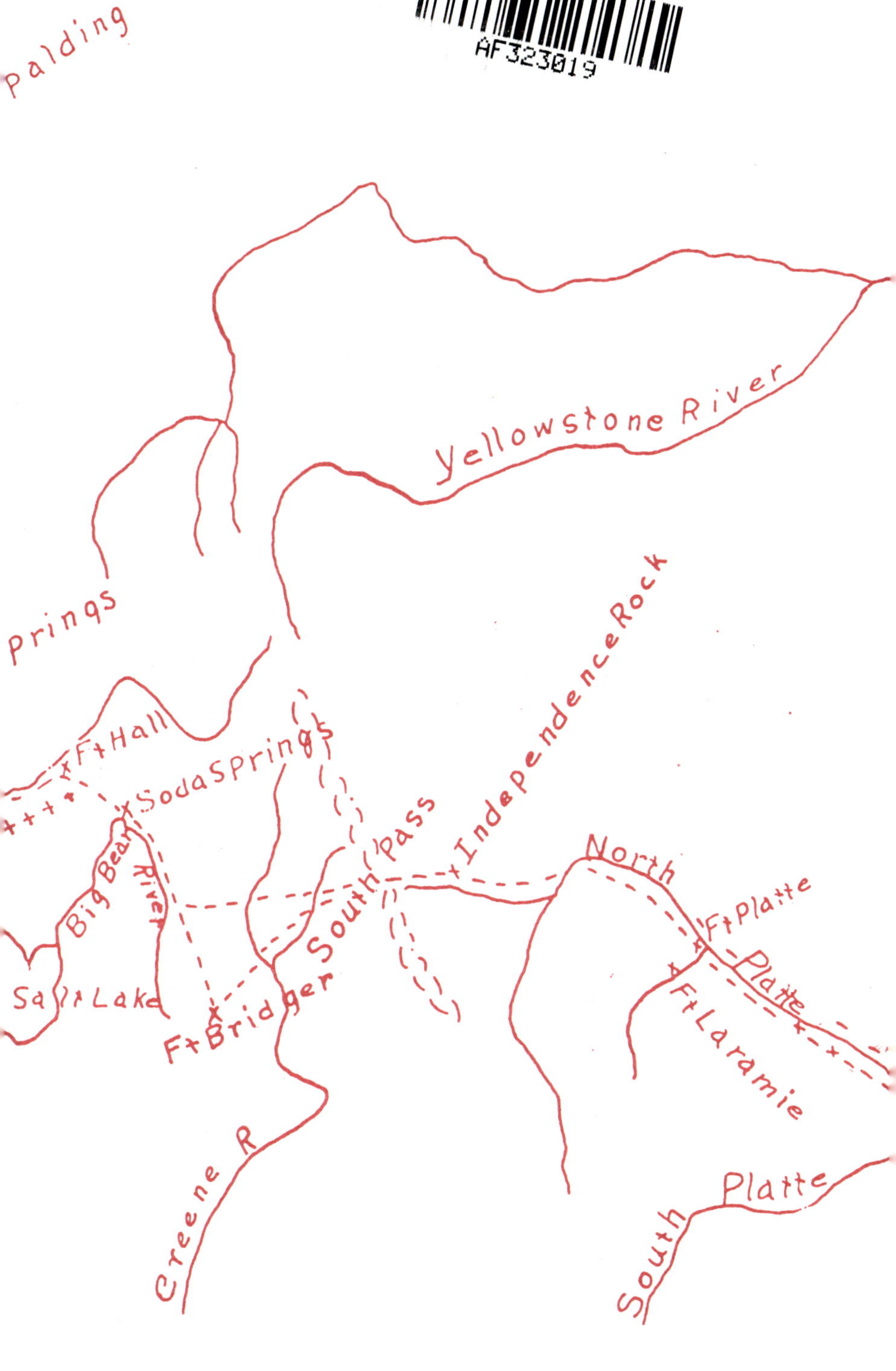

HOW MANY MILES FROM ST. JO?

Clark and his wife

HOW MANY MILES FROM ST. JO?

THE LOG OF STERLING B. F. CLARK
A FORTY-NINER

With comments by Ella Sterling Mighels

YE GALLEON PRESS
FAIRFIELD, WASHINGTON

Library of Congress Cataloging-in-Publication Data

Clark, Sterling B.F., 1825 - 1852.
How many miles from St. Joe?: the log of Sterling B.F. Clark, a forty-niner/ with comments by Ella Sterling Mighels. p. cm.
Reprint. Originally published: San Francisco: priv. print., 1929.
Includes index.
ISBN 0-87770-461-9.
1. West (U.S.) — Description and travel — 1848 - 1860. 2. Overland journeys to the Pacific. 3. California — Gold discoveries. 4. Oregon Trail. 5. California Trail. 6. Clark, Sterling B.F., 1825 - 1852 — Diaries. I. Mighels, Ella Sterling, 1853 - 1934. II. Title.

F593.C58   1988
917.8′042—dc19   88-39052

How Many Miles From St. Jo?

THE LOG OF STERLING B. F. CLARK
A FORTY-NINER

With Comments by Ella Sterling Mighels

TOGETHER WITH

A BRIEF AUTOBIOGRAPHY OF

JAMES PHELAN, 1819–1892

PIONEER MERCHANT

DEDICATED TO
OUR PIONEER FATHERS
AND MOTHERS

CONTENTS

ILLUSTRATIONS

FOREWORD

This bit of intimate California history may interest many who have heretofore considered the "gold-rush" as an event dissociated from the individuals who participated in it. They know something of the vast immigration in mass, but little of the men who trekked to the Land of Gold and of the incidental romance and tragedy such as this story unfolds.

It is reasonable to suppose that most of the venturesome spirits who came to California in '49 had wives or sweethearts at home, and this simple story, while having a pathos of its own, is no doubt typical of the experiences of many, and will serve to bring about a sympathetic understanding and a fuller appreciation of our pioneer ancestors.

After reading the Log of Sterling B. F. Clark, here reproduced for the first time, with comments by his daughter, Ella Sterling Mighels ("Aurora

FOREWORD

Esmeralda"), through whose kindness the manu-script came into my hands, I thought that its publication might elicit personal recollections of other pioneers, handed down by them to their sons and daughters.

The original Log, and the portraits herein reproduced of Clark and his wife, and of his child, are now in the library of the Society of California Pioneers, to which they have been presented for preservation.

In contemplating the fate of Clark, I thought of my own father, who in 1849 barely survived the crossing of the Isthmus of Panama, near where Clark fell; hence I have added his brief autobiography.

JAMES D. PHELAN

San Francisco, December, 1929.

I

THE LOG OF STERLING B. F. CLARK
A FORTY-NINER

INTRODUCTION

HOW Many Miles from St. Jo?" This is the burden of the following story which was chronicled day by day by one of the Forty-Niners who belonged to the Vanguard of the West. Yet it was not from "St. Jo" that this Forty-Niner originally set forth, but from far-off Rutland, about 1200 miles to the eastward in the Green Mountain State.

It was at Rutland, Vermont, that Sterling B. F. Clark was born in 1825, the eighth child of his parents. He was of Revolutionary stock, of New England ancestry on both sides, and a descendant of High Clark who had settled in Connecticut as early as 1640.

One of Vermont's chief industries was quarrying, an industry in which the Clark family extensively engaged; but as many members of the family had died young as a result of inhaling marble-dust, Sterling Clark himself determined to escape from this menace to his line. He therefore took up the study of surveying, printing, and presswork, and educated himself for the profession of teaching, and finally for the law. When thus equipped, he said farewell to marble-cutting and went to Albany, New York, then to New York City, thence to Philadelphia, arriving, at laſt, at Hollidaysburg, Pennsylvania, a town neſtling in the Alleghanies, on the banks of the "Blue Juniata."

Here he became editor of a country paper published nearby at Huntington. Later he taught school in the vicinity. It was at Hollidaysburg that he met Rachel Mitchell, "the lady of his dreams." Rachel Mitchell was a young woman of rare beauty who had twice been chosen by Presidents of the United States to lead the grand march at promenade concerts given at Bedford Springs, the fashionable watering-place of the day. Her father, a Phila-

INTRODUCTION

delphian, was the principal of the Hollidaysburg school, and she assisted him in his work
with the younger pupils, a task for which she
was eminently fitted.

When the news of the discovery of gold in
California flashed over the country, Sterling
Clark resolutely determined to "go West."
Asking Rachel Mitchell "to wait" for him,
he set forth on his long and difficult journey
towards "St. Jo," there to join his fortunes
with the thousands seeking their way to the
Land of Gold.

Here is his Log, which has been preserved
all these years to tell his story and how he
made his way. The Log is reproduced ver-
batim, retaining its spelling of proper names,
changes having been made only as regards
capitalization and punctuation. In the instances
where words have been supplied for the sake
of clearness, such additions have been in-
dicated by brackets.   E. S. M.

THE LOG

MONDAY, March 11[12]th, 1849. Left Hollidaysburg, Pa., 10 o'clock P. M., in company with Captain Joseph Taylor to go to California. Arrived in Pittsburgh, Wednesday morning. (A coach ride, Standard.)

Left Pittsburgh Thursday 15th on board the steamboat Consignee. [Saw] sunk steamboat Caroline. Visited Wheeling, Va., Cincinatti, Ohio. Was tied up to two trees above Cairo. Arrived the 23d at St. Louis. Started next day, Saturday, at noon. Visited Missouri Lodge I. O. O. F. Arrived at St. Joseph 31, Saturday —myself sick and confined to room. Left Pittsburg company; lost ninety-five dollars by it. Joined Evans' Wheeling company. Started 26 Apr. Broke down a/c 3 tongues. Reached Bluffs 27 [28] Apr., Saturday. 7 miles. Broke down, got stuck and helped out 12 or 15 times. Had to unload our wagons 3 or 4 times. Started for Wolf River, 29th. Reached there 1st May. Reached Agency 3 o['clock] Wednesday. Unloaded and started for St. Jo. 21 + 7 = 28 miles.

Reached St. Jo 4 May on Friday.*

Started Tuesday night, 8 May, reached Agency Wednesday, 9 May. Started Thursday, 10. Made 6 miles. 28 + 6 = 32.† Gathered weeds to cook supper and breakfast. Encamped Friday, 11. Started in morning Sunday, after being helped by a friend and four yoke of oxen. Made 7 miles and got stuck again. Had to unload all our wagon. 32 + 7 = 39. Prairie gently rolling. No wood. Very bad water.

(*Ob.*) We have 2 yoke of oxen, 5 mules and a good horse, and yet we balk at every

---

* Evidently, from the Log, a false start was made, as he first arrived at St. Joseph on March 31.

† This, as well as any subsequent errors in additions or calculations of mileage, follows the original manuscript. The corrected total mileage is given in the Summary on page 30.

hard place. Our mess is composed of Evans, Clark, Dubois and Irvine.

The Wheeling company are 3 or 4 days' travel ahead of us, probably 60 or 70 miles. We shall probably have to throw away half of our load before we go two hundred miles further. Pleasant weather. No game yet. Had thunder-shower to-day. Health middling. — (*Vide*). Letter to [name illegible] for laſt 10 days' record.—

Saturday, 12th May. Stuck in one of the ravines or swampy runs of the prairie. Had to unload. Made 14. $39 + 14 = 53$.

Sunday, 13th, made 19 miles. Not much trouble. $53 + 19 = 72$. (*Ob.*) Truly we are now where the flowers spring up unsown and die ungathered and waſte their sweetness on the desert air. Rattlesnakes very plentiful.

Monday, 14th. Very heavy thunder-shower this morning. 4 o'clock P. M. came about 12 miles. $72 + 12 = 84$.

Tuesday, 15th. Made 18 miles. $84+18=$ 102.

Wednesday, 16th. Crossed Nemahaw. Not large. Drove behind the government train 28 miles. $102+28=130$.

Thursday, 17th. Crossed the Big Blue River in morning. Water 3½ ft. deep. Made 18 miles. $130+18=148$.

Friday, 18th. Made 22 miles. Crossed Little Blue. $148+22=170$.

Saturday, 19th. Made 20 miles. Crossed Little Sandy. About 40 have died on this and on the Independence road with a species of cholera. $170+20=190$.

Sunday, 20th. Came 11 miles and encamped at 11 o'clock for the remainder of the day. $11+190=201$.

— Wednesday, 9th of May, at Wolf Creek saw a box in a tree which contained the dead body of an Indian child. —

Monday, 21. Made 21 miles. Came upon

Saturday 19th made 20 miles
crossed little Sandy
about 40 have died on this and
the Independence road with
a species of Cholera
~~[crossed out]~~   170+20=190
Sunday 20th came 11 miles
and encamped at 11 oclock
for ~~[crossed out]~~ the remainder
of the day   11+190=201

Wednesday 4th of May
at wolf creek Saw a boy
in a tree which contained the
dead body of an ~~[crossed out]~~ Indian
Child

Monday 21   made 21 miles
came upon the little blue encamped
at night upon it   21+200(22)
Tuesday 22   made 23 miles
on the bank of the blue and encamped
at night upon it. The road

the Little Blue. Encamped at night upon it. 21 + 201 = 222.

Tuesday, 22. Made 23 miles on the bank of the Blue and encamped at night upon it. The road as far as the eye can reach is one continuous string of wagons. We are travelling now in company with four other wagons, two from Mo. and two from Ill. Passed Government train this night.

No rain of any consequence since last I spoke of the thunder-storm. Weather sometimes very pleasant, constant wind. 23 + 222 = 255.

Wednesday, 23. Left the Little Blue at noon. Encamped without water except what we had in our canteens. Made 20 miles. 255 + 20 = 275.

Thursday, 24. Made 18 miles and encamped upon the Platte. No wood. Violent thunder-storm. Water six inches in the tent. Spent two hours in the vain attempt to build a fire of buffalo chips. Wet, and would not burn. $18 + 275 = 293$.

Friday, 25. Crawled out of our wet beds, cold and shivering. Went 5 miles and took coffee. Went 3 more and encamped upon the Platte. Little wood. 8 miles. $8 + 293 = 301$.

Saturday, 26th. Laid up at Fort Kearney. Coupled our wagon shorter. Dubois left. I disposed of my books. Gave some to Capt. McLane and some to Major Rough, U. S. Army.

Sunday, 27. Started. Made 11 miles. Travelled on the Platte River, and on it encamped. Road perfectly level. $301+11=312$.

Monday, 28. Made 20 miles. Road lying upon the Platte. No wood. Cooked with buffalo chips. $312 + 20 = 332$.

Tuesday, 29. Made 22 miles. Buffalo chips burn well. Road on the Platte. Tremendous thunder-storm during the night. Tent lets through nearly all the rain which falls upon it. $332 + 22 = 354$.

THE LOG

Wednesday, 30. Made 16 miles. Very cold. Laid down at night in dripping wet clothes; wrapped in a wet blanket. Cold wind.

Thursday, 31. Wet, drizzling day. Made 13 miles today on Platte. Very cold. $354 + 13 + 367$. Came upon the South Fork [of the] Platte.

Friday, June 1. Made 23 miles. Pleasant. $367 + 23 = 390$.

Saturday, 2. Went hunting. Saw droves of wolves, three buffaloes, lots of antelope. Killed nothing. Went 20 miles from the road; came near getting lost. Team made 20 miles. Rode a-hunting a mule. Passed fork of the Platte at 4 o'clock. $390 + 20 = 410$.

Sunday, 3d. Went 8 miles and encamped on the South Fork of Platte, where there was wood so that we could wash. Sorry business to the hands. $410 + 8 = 418$.

Monday, 4th. Made 22 miles on the South Fork. Pleasant. $418 + 22 = 440$.

THE LOG

Tuesday, 5. Came 20 miles on South Fork. Crossed it at 4 o'clock and encamped for the night. Width of river nearly ½ mile, 2½ ft. deep, sandy bottom. Thunder-storm at night. 440 + 20 = 460.

Wednesday, 6th. Crossed from the South Fork to the North Fork of the Platte, diſtance 18 miles. (Bryant 22.) Sublime, picturesque scenery when you come within sight of the North Fork, of high bluffs.

Encamped in ash hollow, a deep basin near the river. Seven Indian lodges on river with traders. 460 + 18 = 478.

Thursday, 7th. Came on the south side of the North Fork 18 miles.

Weather pleasant. Indian mode of travelling &c. 478 + 18 = 496.

Friday, 8th. Came 20 miles. 496 + 20 = 516.

Saturday, 9th. Came 21 miles. Passed the Court House [Rock] about four miles from the road. 516 + 21 = 537.

—(*Ob.*) Came in sight of the Chimney Rock* in the morning of the 9th. —

Sunday, 10. Came 9 miles and encamped by the side of the road. All the water near is strongly impregnated with alkali. Will effervesce when an acid is put into it. $537+9=546$. (*Ob.* Thunder-storm 9th at night.)

Monday, 11th. Made 14 miles. At noon resolved to pack the remainder of the way when we should arrive at Fort Laramie, and commenced selling in the afternoon. Left our train. $546+14=560$.

Tuesday, 12. Made 18 miles. Road muddy. Thunder-shower at 2 o'clock, when we reached Scott's Bluff. $560+18=578$.

Wednesday, 13. Left the river and made 20 miles over and through high bluffs. $578+20=598$.

---

* Court House Rock and Chimney Rock are famous landmarks in Western Nebraska. Chimney Rock "is a little west of where the one hundred and third meridian crosses the Platte." Court House Rock stands some distance east of Chimney Rock.

Thursday, 14. Made 20 miles. $598 + 20 = 618$.

Friday, 15. Crossed Laramie's fork and encamped. Sell out and go on pack-mules. 16 miles. $618 + 16 = 634$. Remained at Fort Laramie from Friday, 15th, until Thursday, 21st, when we started on pack[-mules]. By mistake I got separated from my mess and company. Staid all night with Major Henley & Field and Jackson. Next day, Friday 22, went in pursuit of my mess. Could not find them. Returned, bought another mule and made arrangements to go in company with Henley & Co.

Sunday, 24th. Started and made 24 miles. $24 + 634 = 658$.

Monday, 25. Made 14 miles. $658 + 14 = 672$. (*Ob.*) Great trouble in packing. Sick five or six days with the diarhoea.

Tuesday, 26. Came 28 [miles]. $672 + 28 = 700$.

THE LOG

Wednesday, 27. Crossed La Bonta. Made ⁻30 miles. 700+30=730.

Thursday, 28. Crossed rivers A La Prole, branch Boise & Deer Creek and came upon the North Fork of the Platte 5 miles before crossing Deer River. Diſtance 23 miles. 730 +23=753. (*Ob.*) Our road has been now, since leaving Fort Laramie, over the Black Hills, a barren country with but very little grass. Had to go six miles out from the road for grass.

Friday, 29. Came to the ferry of the Platte, crossed and encamped on the north side. Distance 20 miles. 753+20=773.

Saturday, June 30. Road over hills strongly impregnated with alkali. Encamped 2 miles east of Willow Spring. 26 miles. 773+26 =799.

July 1. Passed (Sunday) Independence Rock. Crossed Sweetwater River. Made 37 miles. 799+37=836.

THE LOG

Mon., July 2nd. Road over Alkali Springs and swamp. Dead oxen strew the way. 31 miles. Sweetwater ford No. 4. 836+31=867.

Tues., July 3. 21 miles on Sweetwater. 867+21=888.

Wedn., 4th. 20 miles. 13 miles east of the summit of the South Pass of the Rocky Mountains encamped. 888+13=901.

Thurs., 5. Crossed the summit and encamped on the Dry Sandy. 23 miles. 924.

Friday, 6. Passed the junction of the Oregon and California roads and encamped on the Big Sandy. 22 miles. 946.

Saturday, 7th. Came onto Big Sandy again. North to Green River. 27 miles. 973.

Sunday, 8th. Ferried over the river in the morning. Made 5 miles. 978.
—(NOTE) Snow on the mountains; came upon banks from 8 to 15 feet deep. Water froze in our canteens at night on the mountains. Air more pleasant, and warmer after crossing the

mountains. The ground strongly alkaline. —

Monday, 9th. Came 34 miles. Stopped at night upon the Black Fork. $978 + 34 = 1012$.

Tuesday, 10. Came 21 miles and reached Fort Bridger. Encamped in the bottom. 1033.

Wednesday, 11. Staid at Fort Bridger. Got mules shod. (Snake Indians.)

Thursday, 12. Made 14 miles. 1047. Travelling in company with a Missouri train of ox-wagons.

Friday, 13th. Went 19 miles in the same co[mpany]. 1066.

Saturday, 14. Left the train and made 26 miles. 1092.

Sunday, 15th. Made 28 miles up mountains. Rough road. 1120.

Monday, 16. Made 27 miles. Reached Salt Lake City. 1147.

Tuesday, 17. Laid up.

Wednesday, 18. Laid up.

Thursday, 19. Still at Salt Lake City.

Stopped and boarded at Teft's. Bathed twice in warm springs.

Friday, 20. Started at 11 o'clock A. M., and came 40 miles to the Weber River. Arrived at 12 o'clock. 1187.

Saturday, 21. Made 28 miles to Box Elder. 1215.

Sunday, 22. Made 21 miles. Crossed Bear River. Ferried. Stopped on Malad Creek. 1236.

Monday, 23. Made 32 miles to spring in the mountains, twelve miles after leaving warm springs. 1268.

Tuesday, 24. Passed spring in the plains. Made 26 miles. 1394.

Wednesday, 25. Arrived at Caggeen Creek. 28 miles. 1422.

Thursday, 26. Joined Fort Hall road. Goose Creek. Steeple Rocks. 25 miles. 1447.

Friday, 27. Up Goose Creek and 2 miles beyond. 25 miles. 1472.

Saturday, 28. Crossed the dividing ridge

between Oregon and California into Hot Spring Valley. Made 26 miles. 1498.

Sunday, 29. Left valley, came upon the headwaters of a branch of Humboltd River. Made 29 miles. 1527.

Monday, 30. Made 28 miles. Struck Humboltd River 2½ miles before camping. 1555.

Tuesday, 31. Made 27 miles on Humboltd River. 1582.

Wednesday, August 1. Took a cut-off. Followed the river. Travelled at night. 29. 1611.

Thursday, 2. Came over the hills to Mary's River. (2 miles on river.) 23 miles. 1634.

Friday, 3d. On Humboltd River. Made 29 miles. 1663.

Saturday, 4th. Made 28 miles. 1691.

Sunday, 5. Made 20 miles. 1711.

Monday, 6th. Made 27 miles. 1738.

Tuesday, 7th. Made 26 miles. 1764.

Wednesday, 8. Made 28 miles on Humboltd. Camped on Willows, Echo and Bluffs. Lost canteen. 1792.

— The road on Humboltd very sandy and heavy, increasing as you go down the river; the air conſtantly filled with the dust. —

Thursday, 9. Left in the morning and went 12 miles down the river to find good grass. Stopped till next morning at 2 o'clock. 1804.

Friday, 10. Made 12 miles to the slough for breakfaſt; to the left 6 miles for grass. Remained till the next morning. 1816.

Saturday, 11. Started in morning to cross the desert. Went 25 miles, 5 beyond the sink of the river, where we stopped and got some supper. Started at 6 o'clock. Went 17 miles by 11 o'clock, then fed the little hay which I had packed on my pack-mule and slept an hour. Started at one o'clock. 1858.

Sunday, 12. Went 13 miles and ſtopped to rest ½ hour. Started on the last 10 miles at sunrise. One mule gave out and we had to leave him. Went it very slow, but came to river nearly exhausted, having come 68 miles in less than 24 hours without water, except sulphur water, which would vomit us by the smell. 1881.

Monday, August 13. Went 17 miles on Salmon Trout River. 1881.

Tuesday, 14. Went 28 miles on river. 1909.

Wednesday, 15. 29 miles made. Struck and made 18 miles in Salmon Trout River Valley. Rich soil and timber upon the west side up the mountains. 1938.
—We have been gradually ascending and getting among the Sierra Nevada Mountains.—

Thursday, 16. Made in the forenoon in the valley 19 miles and struck Pass Creek leading through the mountains, which will make the valley 37 miles long. By looks it is from 6 to 10 miles wide.

THE LOG

Afternoon. Up the canon [canyon] 5 miles,
and 6 miles to a small valley, where camped.
Diſtance 30 miles. Road horrible. Wagons
broken. 1968.

Friday, 17. Last night was one continuous
series of thunder-showers which laſted until
to-day at 10 o'clock. Started in the rain and
went in the forenoon to Lake Valley, 11 miles,
through snow, hail and wind. Stopped in the
pleasant sun to dry and get dinner.

Afternoon. Over the highest ridge, over
snow-drifts 20 feet deep, freezing cold. Steep
perpendicular rocks. On the rocks in the
mountains were left broken 26 wagons. At
night cold, freezing. Diſtance 10 miles. Whole
diſtance 21. 1989.

Saturday, 18th. Started [in] morning and
came 12 miles to Lost Spring, and on to Camp
Creek, down ridges, [through] heavy timber,
come 9 miles, and on 16 miles down ridge.
Overtaken by night in an attempt to follow a

track from the road down to a valley for grass. An hour's fruitless attempt to find the track exhausted our worn bodies, and so we camped in the woods, tying our horses to trees, having eat nothing since morning. Diſtance 37 miles. 2026.

Sunday, 19th. Found a path and went 2 miles to valley to lay up to grass. Got breakfast. Laid up.

Monday, 20th. Left grass and went to the Gold Diggins. 21 miles. Stopped with Irvine all night. 2047.

Tuesday, 21. Went 18 miles towards Sacramento City. 2065.

Wednesday, 22. Went 20 miles; within 5 miles of the city. Sent my baggage to Colloma by Bean & Barnes. 2087.

Thursday, 23. Went to city, 5 miles. Staid till night. Went with Werner to camp across the Sacramento. The city is juſt below the confluence of the Sacramento & American rivers, mostly built of cloth houses, about 700 in number. Population 3500; 3 months old. 2092.

Friday, 24. Went to town. Saw [New York] Herald [dated] 30 June. Heard of the attack upon Rome by the French, Polk's death, &c.

Saturday, 25. In camp.

Sunday, 26. In camp.

Monday, 27. Went to Sacramento. Sold my mule for $50. Bought mining tools, &c. Went out 5 miles.

Tuesday, 28. Camped 7 miles from Mormon Island.

Wednesday, 29. Went to Island and prospected.

Thursday, 30. Went 12 miles up the American Fork to the Sandwich Island diggings & prospected.

Friday, 31. Came back to Mormon Island.

Saturday, Sep. 1. Commenced gold washing.

Sunday, 2. [No entry.]

THE LOG

[Separately in the Log, the following observations were entered by its author:]

Fort Laramie
>Lat.   42° 12' 13"
>Lon. 104° 11' 53"
>Alt. 4090

Summit South Pass Rocky Mountains
>Lat.   42° 18' 58"
>Long. 4 miles east of 108° 40'
>Alt.   7085

Fort Bridger
>Lat.   41° 19' 13"
>Long. 110° 5'
>Alt.   6665

Mountain before descending to Salt Lake City from which you have a view of the valley of Salt Lake, 20 miles east of valley.
>A 7245

Mormon City

    Lat. $40°\ 45'\ 44''$

    Lon. $111°\ 26'\ 34''$

    Alt. 4300

    Sulphur Hot Springs

Variation of Magnetic Needle $15°\ 47'\ 23''$ East.

Settlements [No entry.]

SUMMARY

THE following Summary of the route travelled by Clark has been compiled by the editor from the Log:

March, 1849: Hollidaysburg, Pittsburgh, Pa., St. Joseph.

April: St. Louis, Mo., Council Bluffs, Wolf River, Agency, St. Joseph.

May: Nemahah, Little Blue, Little Sandy, Platte, Fort Kearney, South Fork Platte.

June: North Fork, Court House Rock, Fort Laramie, A La Prole, Branch Boise and Deer Creek, Black Hills, Wilson Spring.

July: Independence Rock, Sweetwater River, Alkali Springs, South Pass Rocky Mountains, Dry Sandy, Junction Oregon and California roads, Green River, Black Fork, Fort Bridger,

SUMMARY

Salt Lake City, Weber River, Box Elder, Bear River, Malad Creek, Caggeen Creek, Fort Hall Road, Goose Creek, Steeple Rocks, Hot Spring Valley, Humboldt River.

August: Mary's River, Willows, Echo and Bluffs, Salmon Trout River, Salmon Trout River Valley, Sierra Nevada Mountains, Pass Creek, Lost Spring, Camp Creek.

Gold Diggings, Sacramento City, Mormon Island, Sandwich Island Diggings.

Including 28 miles recorded for the false start from St. Joseph, the Log shows a total of 2022 miles travelled from St. Joseph to California.

AFTERMATH

HERE ends the Log of this earnest Forty-Niner. It made no difference whether there was anything to eat or not, nor whether the snow lay across his path twenty feet deep or not, he had to record each day just how many miles he had gone and add it to the miles travelled from "St. Jo." Other men might write of scenery, or of Indians and bears, or of quarrels en route. Not so with Sterling B. F. Clark of Vermont. He permitted nothing to interfere with his knowing just how far he had gone each day. Yet, tied up in the treasured package containing this faithful record were letters from the same hand to "the girl he left behind him" in Hollidaysburg, Blair County, Pennsylvania, in which appear the same persistent devotion and the same determination to win that he showed in fighting through to California. California, beautiful and glorious as she was, was not enough for him. He also wanted the "beauteous lady of his heart." He wanted her to leave her Eastern home and join him here. For he had prospered and had invested his money in land in Sacramento and San Jose, and had been appointed to office, becoming "Alcalde" Clark for Natoma, or Mormon Island, as it was later called.

The following extracts from letters written to Rachel Mitchell by Clark continue the story.

EXTRACTS FROM LETTER WRITTEN IN 1850:

One year ago to-night at this very hour, I was one hundred and fifty miles west of Salt Lake crossing the desert, my mouth parched with thirst, and myself speechless, without the first desire to live and without expectation of ever reaching the spring in the mountains which might save me. And here to-night I am writing from California to her who has

just assured me by letter that her love is as
conſtant as mine, and if it be as conſtant as
I believe it to be pure, in a few months more
I shall meet her once again, never more to
part. . . .

It seems as though my affeċtion for you
increases every day, for there is hardly an
hour, while awake, but that I find myself at-
tempting to depiċt and piċture to my mind a
scene which I imagine will be the happieſt of
my life: the time when I shall return to strike
glad hands with you. . . .

I am pleased to hear of your ſtudies and
improvement in music with the guitar and the
piano. I was just looking at your minature,
and a thought occured to my mind which has
presented itself a thousand times. How ever
more lovely you would look if you would part
your raven-black hair upon the top and comb
it both ways down, inſtead of drawing some
of it backward from the front to the back. I

have only time to say that you have surpassed yourself in this laſt letter, it being the nonpareil of all the thousand-and-one letters you have written to me, in your final saying that you are willing to leave your home in Pennsylvania and that you wish to live in California.

There does not a day pass but that my imagination piĉtures to my mind the happy time in anticipation of meeting you, and delivering into your possession that which I have already given — my hand and heart, and claiming yours in return. The letter before me has occasioned me more joy and delight than could be told in an oĉtavo — it has transported me, and I go about my business with a lightsome heart and a glad countenance. Believe me, language cannot express with what affeĉtion and truth I write, forever yours,

STERLING*

* "*Literary California.*" By Ella Sterling Mighels. P. 175. (Harr Wagner Publishing Co., San Francisco, 1918.)

AFTERMATH

As for this country being backward like all other new countries, it is a mistake. It is as far (if not farther) advanced in literature, science and the arts as any State in the Union. There is more talent in the cities and in the mines of California than in any of the older States. This may seem a broad assertion, but it is nevertheless true.

We have many weddings here, even though the outside world considers that we are semi-barbarous. I have married two couples myself, since I became Alcalde. The fact of it is this: nothing in this country is the same as it is in the States. Everything is changed—man's nature even! I am no more the same person. It cannot be expressed in words—no power of language can portray or convey a correct idea of the state of life in California. There are no laws, but very few crimes are committed. Gambling and intemperance reign supreme, but there is little drunkeness or dishonesty, and the great cause of these anomalies is mostly FEAR. If a man does wrong, we hang him at once. If one trespasses upon the rights of another, he shoots him and— that ends it. So that everyone counts well the cost before he engages in anything doubtful.

As I have sat under a tree on a Sabbath listening to the preacher, I have wished for the genius of a painter to transfer to canvas the scene that presented itself. The minister is near at hand, praying; near at hand [also] sounds the auctioneer crying, "Going, going, gone!" Then comes from the gambling tables, "Twenty-five on the king?" Then the woodsman's ax is heard; next, "Whoa, gee up there, go 'long" from the driver of an ox-team. And amid all this din of medley sound voices of heterogeneous beings in conglomerated variety of pursuits and chaotic antagonisms. How strange that there should be anything like

AFTERMATH

order! And yet everything moves harmoni-
ously!

Sterling B. F. Clark*

The following letter, written in mucilage
on blue letter-paper and sprinkled with gold-
dust and small nuggets of gold, was sent by
Clark to Rachel Mitchell on her birthday. In
June, 1929, a descendant of theirs preserved
this letter between glass for the future. It is in
a remarkable ſtate of preservation, the gold-
duſt virtually intaċt.

Natoma, Sep. 12th, '50
Midnight

Dear Rachel:

The next mail leaves this city on the 14th,
and I have only time to write a few lines. My
health is good as usual. Time passes rapidly
here. Very soon a few months will have passed
away, and very soon shall I be by your side,

* Ibid. P. 111.

to enjoy that happy scene which bright anticipation now pictures to my mind.

Write as soon as you receive this.

As always   STERLING*

Rachel   P. S. Excuse brevity.

These letters, continuing for several years,
show that Sterling Clark's entreaties at laſt
prevailed: the lovely young woman would be
willing to live in California — but he muſt return to the Eaſt for her, as her father was not
willing that she undertake the journey alone.

Clark ventured all. He went to San Francisco, bought beautiful crepe shawls, gold
bracelets and other gifts for the bride that
was to be, as well as for relatives back in
Rutland. He spent thousands of dollars on this
trip, putting through all that he had planned.
He went via Panama to New York and visited
both Pennsylvania and Vermont.

* Original in possession of Ella Sterling Clark Mighels.

AFTERMATH

And at laſt, these two embarked for California via Nicaragua, leaving all the Eaſt behind them. Sterling Clark might be able to breaſt the snows and the sands and the sulphur of the plains on his overland journey, but the miasma of Nicaragua was a far worse danger. On his journey Eaſt, he had become affected, and on his return the Lake of Nicaragua exacted the last tribute of his ſtrength. Arriving in San Francisco, he was carried from the ship to the Rassette House on a ſtretcher. Two weeks later, the young bride was left a widow, and the young Forty-Niner, then 28 years old, was laid to reſt in Yerba Buena Cemetery. Ten years later his body was removed to Lone Mountain, and it now reposes in Mountain View Cemetery, Oakland.

When Mrs. Sterling B. F. Clark arrived at the mining camp in her deep mourning, she created a sensation. Men and women, alike, greeted her sorrowfully. In settling the eſtate, moſt of the property was awarded by the Court to the widow and to the poſthumous child that was to be, two lots in Sacramento, where the Capitol and the Governor's Mansion now ſtand, being particularly set apart and the title veſted in the unborn child.

Seven months after Sterling B. F. Clark's death, his daughter was born, and every man and woman in the town welcomed the fatherless babe. All came with gifts, and not to be outdone, some miners from the American River brought a gold-rocker, converted it into a cradle and took turns in rocking her to sleep. That was in May, 1853.

Times have changed. A new order of things claims us. Nevertheless, deep feelings are stirred within us when dwelling on these tales of the paſt. Since then, this Native Daughter of the Golden Weſt has twice passed over the Iſthmus of Panama. Twelve times has she

Clark's Posthumous Child

crossed the Continent; and always, when passing the Wahsatch Mountains which loom so wondrously, she dwells on the memory of that father of hers who passed this way "In the Vanguard of the West."

Who can fail to be thrilled by the thought of one man alone in this vastness of nature — left behind sometimes when ill—amid thunder-storms or twenty feet of snow, missing his party, getting on his mule, joining a new party, going on his way once more! Wondering, without doubt, whether he would ever see Rachel again.

And how glad we are that he did see her again, even though she was soon to be a bride in widow's weeds, left to mourn him! No story of the early days is more tragic, more pathetic, more interesting than this one which begins recording the number of miles from "St. Jo."

E. S. M.

II

BRIEF AUTOBIOGRAPHY
OF JAMES PHELAN, 1819-1892
PIONEER MERCHANT

James Phelan

JAMES PHELAN

WHEN I heard the ſtory of California gold, I was incredulous, and waited for confirmatory news. This I received in the published report of Thomas O. Larkin, United States Consul at Monterey, made to James Buchanan, then Secretary of State. I immediately saw the advantage to the merchant, shipped three cargoes of diversified merchandise to the port of San Francisco and personally took passage to the Iſthmus of Panama in order that I might arrive before my shipments. But, while on the Isthmus, I was ſtricken with the deadly Chagres fever. For a long time I lay amidſt miserable surroundings, and I fully expeéted, in common with many others, gradually to lose my ſtrength and die.

It seemed a hopeless ſtruggle, but by singular good fortune Dr. Carpenter, subsequently a fellow member of the Society of California Pioneers, tenderly cared for me until I was able to get on my feet. I was so weak, however, that I often despaired of ever reaching the Golden Gate. The steamship office was besieged for passage to San Francisco by the men on the Isthmus, but all applications were refused. There were, it was said, no accommodations. Everyone was advised to wait patiently until ships arrived which would adequately take care of the increased numbers stranded in that infested land. I do not believe I could have remained there for a very long time without succumbing. Finally, besieged by a hostile mob, the agent of the historic steamship "Panama" posted a bulletin informing us all that there were two cabins and three steerage accommodations on that ship, which was due to arrive in a very short time. In order to placate the multitude, he proposed to have all of the registered applicants draw lots. I drew a steerage ticket, and Dr. Carpenter prepared me for the voyage. But I soon discovered that the ſteerage was no place for a sick man and I then had to resort to ſtrategy.

On board were many supplies which I had sent from the East by quick dispatch, and of which I apprised the purser. He said the ship's galley required a quantity of saleratus and asked if I would be willing to sell some of this much needed commodity. I had divined the character of supplies which would be moſt in demand in a new land, and felt I was in possession of something very valuable, but so sick was I that I told him I would give him whatever he wanted, provided he would only give me more comfortable accommodations. I believe the shift saved my life.

Safely we arrived in port after a rough voyage up the coaſt, and I soon recuperated my health in the bracing atmosphere of San

Francisco, now famous for the salubrity of its summers; for this was in the month of August —August, 1849.

One of the ships carrying my supplies went down at sea, but the other two arrived in good season, and with these shipments I soon set up a thriving trade with the mines; but twice my warehouse and ſtore were deſtroyed by fire. In those days the merchants clubbed together and insured themselves, each individual name being upon each policy, because there were no other facilities; so my loss was not a total one.

The lack of communication and the delay of transportation made business fascinating in those days. It was unlike modern commerce, where everything is known, and where the need is determined before the order is given. The pioneer merchants had to use their judgment as to the wisdom of importation —by one route or another —of commodities which were salable. If you were ahead of your competitors, they could not profit because of your foresight. Frequently, cargoes were loſt, but just as bills of exchange were loſt, but made more secure by issuing duplicates and triplicates covering the same items, so it was with shipments.

About that time, the United States offered for sale, at auction, its condemned government ſtores at Benicia. By reason of my acquaintance with John V. Plume, of the banking firm of Burgoyne & Company, who had been a fellow-passenger on the ſteamship "Panama," I was able to borrow seventy thousand dollars for the purpose of acquiring these ſtores, which I accomplished. I soon established connections with the mines, and business thrived.

· After a while, the hard and exacting life of a pioneer merchant led me to abandon business and take up finance, to that end I organized in 1871 and was the first president of the First National Bank of San Francisco. I also helped to organize the Firemans Fund and other insurance companies, besides a company to dredge the Panama Canal, all of which enterprises were successful. In addition to these activities, I took the advice of experienced men (I was only just past twenty-five years of age when I came to California) who observed that as there never could be any more land, and as population was increasing all of the time, it would be profitable to buy real estate, and I never was without resources of that kind, which I believed had the greatest stability.

In 1855 I felt in sufficiently comfortable circumstances to return to Brooklyn, New York, to claim my bride, who was Miss Alice Kelly, the daughter of Jeremiah Kelly and Jane Mulhall Kelly, of Stradbally, Queens County, Ireland. Her uncle was Burrows Kel-

Alice Phelan
wife of James Phelan

ly, Esquire, a famous barrister of Queens County, Ireland, and, on her mother's side, her first cousin was William J. Corbet, Member of Parliament, from the County Wicklow, Ireland, a well-known publicist and poet.

But my trip was interrupted. I was forced back "across the plains," by stage-coach and river boat, in great haste—a journey of great hardship,—because of the receipt of news that my brother, who was my business partner, had, by unfortunate investments, practically wrecked our firm; and I had to begin over again.

Miss Kelly soon after came to San Francisco, via the same perilous Panama route. She was chaperoned by the distinguished United States Senator Joseph Lane, of Oregon, and Representative in Congress Lafayette Grover, who were family friends, and whom she always held in grateful remembrance. We were happily married in May, 1859, in old St.

JAMES PHELAN

Mary's Cathedral, on the corner of California and Dupont Streets, by Archbishop Joseph Sadoc Alemany, the venerable pioneer prelate, and took up our residence in San Francisco, where our three children, Alice, James D., and Mary Louise, were born.

Note: James Phelan died in 1892, aged 74 years, and Alice Phelan died ten years later; they now rest in the family mausoleum at Holy Cross Cemetery, San Mateo County.

APPENDIX

APPENDIX

The following extract and footnote are from volume VIII of Bancroft's History of California, page 169:

"Men preferred to speculate at great odds rather than endure irksome stagnation, and stoical as to the immediate results, they were ever buoyed by the hope of a happy turn. They met the mockery of change with cheerful energy and recuperative power, and if overwhelmed one moment by sweeping financial crash or obliterating conflagration, they were on their feet the next, planning fresh undertakings, and constructing new buildings."

The footnote reads as follows:

"Hawley . . . writes* that he was burned out six times within less than a year and a half; and Neall †
. . . four times within 14 months. Of course, many succumbed. James Phelan was engaged in trade at

* David N. Hawley: "*Observations of Men and Things.*" Manuscript in the Bancroft Library, University of California, Berkeley, California.

† James Neall: "*Vigilance Committee.*" Manuscript in the Bancroft Library.

APPENDIX

Cincinnati when the gold fever induced him to transfer his general merchandise to San Francisco, and there establish himself in August, 1849, with his brother, under the firm J. & M. Phelan, for which a third brother,* John, a merchant in N[ew] York, acted as Atlantic agent. Fires and mismanagement by partners made inroads in time, but Mr. Phelan turned to the rescue and continued as sole trader till 1869, to devote himself to his interest in banking and real estate, the latter distributed in different sections of the coast, and including one of the most conspicuous buildings in S[an] F[rancisco]. In 1870 he helped to organize the first national bank, as president, acting also as director of the national bank of San José. He also participated in forming the Western Fire and Marine Insurance Co., and in pushing operations on the Panama Canal. By all who knew him he was acknowledged as one of the most enterprising of our Cal[ifornia] pioneers, and as one to whom the State was indebted for much of its early prosperity."

*See Swasey: "*The Early Days and Men of California.*" Page 319. Pacific Press Publishing Co., 1891.

COLOPHON

The Sterling B.F. Clark, HOW MANY MILES FROM ST. JOE? *was printed in the workshop of Glen Adams, which is located in the sleepy country village of Fairfield, southern Spokane County in Washington state and one township removed from the Idaho line. This is an enlarged facsimile of the privately printed 1929 edition. Over the intervening 59 years this item has become increasingly scarce. A limited amount of typesetting was done by Pat Nigh using a Compugraphic Editwriter. Photography/darkroom work was by Heather LaTendresse and Vern Stevens using a 20x24 inch DS computer driven camera and a 25 inch LogE automatic film developing machine. The film was stripped by Heather LaTendresse and Vern Stevens. Plates were done by Vern Stevens. Printing was done by Vern Stevens using a 28 inch Heidelberg press, model KORS. Folding was done by Garry Adams using a 22x28 three stage Baum folding machine. Assembly was by Ivadell Chamberlain. The hard case copies were bound by Willem Bosch of Oakesdale, Washington, assisted by his son, Gerrit Bosch. The books were sewn by Juanita Hurlbert using a National book sewing machine. The paper stock is 70 pound Island Offset, a Canadian sheet. This was a fun project. We had no special difficulty with the work.*

Yellowstone River
IndependenceRock
SodaSprings
Big Bear
River
South Pass
North
Ft Platte
Scott's Bl
Platte
Chim
Ft Bridger
Ft Laramie
Ore
Greene R
South Platte